SIGNIFICANT PEOPLE FROM HISTORY

Jacques Cousteau

BASED ON THE BOOK

Who Was Jacques Cousteau?

by Nico Medina

Guide Written by Liam Bredberg

blackbird&company
EDUCATIONAL PRESS

Visit us at

blackbirdandcompany.com

Explore our full range of Discovery guides:

....

Hatchling: Reading | Writing | Phonics

Earlybird: Literature & Writing

Literature & Writing

Storymaker

One True Sentence

Operation Lexicon

Intro to Composition

Exploring Poetry

Research Science

Research History

Printed in the U.S.A.

First Printing, 2020

ISBN 978-1-953357-11-3

V1 01 Nov 2020

SKU: 20-57113

www.blackbirdandcompany.com

Table of Contents

Introduction

What's in a name? The history of the human race is in names. Our objective friends do not understand that, since they move in a world of objects which can be counted and numbered. They reduce the great names of the past to dust and ashes. This they call scientific history. But the whole meaning of history is in the proof that there have lived people before the present time whom it is important to meet.

EUGEN ROSENSTOCK-HUESSY

How This Guide is Organized

Guide Sections - *overview*

This guide is divided into 5 weekly sections:

SECTIONS 1–3

The first three sections each cover a period of the individual's life through the following elements:

Reading
» Weekly reading assignment to begin each section.

Character Lexicon
» Character traits to define and use in original sentences.

Comprehension
» Questions to reinforce observation and understanding.

Writing (BODY – 1st DRAFT)
» Structured paragraphs to begin building the body of the essay.

SECTION 4

Writing (OPENING/CLOSING – 1st DRAFT)
» Structured paragraphs to open and close the essay.

Writing (COMPLETED ESSAY – FINAL DRAFT)
» Combine opening, closing, and body to form the complete essay.

SECTION 5

Culminating Project
» Ideas to further explore and creatively express related topics.

✱ SUPPLEMENTAL READING

The included supplemental reading can be done at anytime along the way. Encourage students to read all they can to help give a fuller picture of the people they are learning about.

How This Guide is Organized (cont.)

Guide Sections - *details*

Assignment Checklist

This form is to be used by both the student and the teacher. Encourage your student to utilize this as a time management device and have them mark off each element as it is completed. The teacher can then comment, evaluate, and grade each element. Depending on the student's learning style and classroom logistics, each element can be evaluated individually or each section can be evaluated when all its elements are complete. On the following pages we have included sample grading and writing guidelines to assist you.

Reading

These research guides are designed to explore the life of a real person. When exploring non-fiction information it is important to seek out multiple sources. We have provided a core and a supplemental reading source for this purpose. Supplemental reading can often be completed in one sitting. Longer supplemental reading should be paced parallel to core reading. This reading provides additional details students can utilize in their essays. We understand that people read, experience, and absorb stories in many different ways and at different rates. However, we recommend students read through each assignment in one sitting before moving on. Keeping the flow of a story intact should be a priority. Therefore, we encourage students to set aside a substantial block of time for reading each week.

Character Lexicon

Exploring and describing the traits of the character is the first element encountered in the guide after reading. This element is the preliminary research that will contribute to the crafting of an original essay. It is designed to help students develop impressions and opinions as they explore traits that each of these remarkable men and women from history possess. As students define and consider the vocabulary words, they will discover a lexicon of traits unique to each of these exemplary individuals. Students will then apply and utilize the lexicon to communicate, through an essay, what they have discovered.

Comprehension

Following the *Character Lexicon* section is a series of questions that will help students engage in the art of crafting complex sentences as they gather specific details of each character's life. Answering questions in complete sentences is good practice, as it reinforces clear thinking and writing skills. It may be helpful for some students to survey the questions before beginning the reading assignment, however, they should not be answered until the reading assignment has been completed so as to maintain continuity while reading. Encouraging students to refer to the book and to note page numbers as they complete the *Comprehension* section is a useful research skill, especially if the guide is used in group settings where information will be discussed.

Writing

The writing assignment is intended to make the reader think, respond and apply, with the added challenge of producing a well crafted, articulate answer. More specifically, this element consists of a directed writing assignment that will culminate in a biographical essay. Beginning with topic wheels to help students organize information gleaned during research, the writing element will guide them through all the stages of the process necessary to craft a unique communication of the historical figure.

This element introduces and reinforces the process of writing, helping students to transform abstract thoughts and ideas into tangible words, sentences, and paragraphs. Writing a rough draft is the first step in completing the assignment. The student should then self-edit the rough draft as much as possible with the usual checks for spelling, grammar, and punctuation, while also paying attention to readability, clarity, and creativity. The student should also conference with their teacher at this time. In *Section 4*, the rough drafts will be combined and rewritten as the final draft, incorporating all edits for a clean and polished essay.

Culminating Project

The creative project should be inspired by something that sparked interest or excited you. Use this opportunity to create something tangible and memorable from the reading that will inspire others.

Writing Guidelines

Five Elements of the Essay - *overview*

Each completed essay will include the following:

1. **Opening Paragraph** (WRITTEN IN SECTION 4)
   » Open your essay with a *Hook*, a *Context Sentence*, and a *Thesis Statement*.

2. **Topic Paragraph 1** (WRITTEN IN SECTION 1)
   » An expanded paragraph developed from *Topic Wheel 1*.

3. **Topic Paragraph 2** (WRITTEN IN SECTION 2)
   » An expanded paragraph developed from *Topic Wheel 2*.

4. **Topic Paragraph 3** (WRITTEN IN SECTION 3)
   » An expanded paragraph developed from *Topic Wheel 3*.

5. **Closing Paragraph** (WRITTEN IN SECTION 4)
   » Close your essay with a *Weave*, an *Echo*, and a *Twist*.

Writing Guidelines (cont.)

Five Elements of the Essay - *details*

1. Opening Paragraph:

Hook
The *Hook* is the first sentence of your essay, the singular sentence that will grab your reader's attention.

Context Sentence
The *Context Sentence* is the sentence that moves the reader from the *Hook* to the *Thesis*.

Thesis Statement
The *Thesis Statement* is a single sentence that introduces readers to the main ideas of your research.

Example Opening Paragraph (writing about Louisa May Alcott)

(Hook)   *Little Women* might be the first thought that comes to mind when asked about author Louisa May Alcott, but when it comes to considering her life, there was nothing little about this woman.

(Context)   This was a writer who brought a diverse experience to her stories, having been a servant, a seamstress, and a Civil War nurse.

(Thesis)   Lousia May Alcott wrote what she knew, and her wonderful stories weave together history and her personal experience, capturing the imagination of readers.

2—4. Topic Paragraphs

Topic Wheel
Topic Wheels help you organize your thoughts and focus on significant details that you wish to communicate. First *Brainstorm* single words or short phrases that might work for the *Topic Wheel*, then complete each spoke of the *Topic Wheel* by choosing the best ideas that describe, expand, and add interest to your topic. Each spoke will be the foundation of one complete sentence. Together, all of the spokes will form the supporting sentences of your *Topic Paragraph*.

5. Closing Paragraph

Weave
The *Weave* is the first sentence of your closing paragraph. This is the sentence that will help your reader begin to come to a close.

Echo
The *Echo* is the sentence that moves the reader from the *Weave* to the *Twist*.

Twist
The *Twist* is a single sentence that closes your essay and leaves readers with an idea that will keep them thinking on your topic.

Example Closing Paragraph

(Weave)   Considering the fact that Louisa May Alcott lived nearly 200 years ago, in a specific time and place, it is remarkable that her writing is so engaging to a diverse audience.

(Echo)   This woman was a remarkable writer.

(Twist)   Lousia May Alcott was not a little woman, but rather a woman with big ideas.

Writing Guidelines (cont.)

Five Stages of the Writing Process - *overview*

As you write, keep in mind the 5 steps that lead to excellent work:

1. **Topic Brainstorm**
   » Think about it. Come up with great ideas for your Topic Wheel.

2. **First Draft**
   » Get your thoughts organized and on paper.

3. **Conference**
   » Carefully read your first draft, have someone else read it and offer input.

4. **Edit/Polish**
   » Check spelling, grammar, content, and style. Make desired changes.

5. **Final Draft**
   » Copy your work using your best penmanship.

Writing Guidelines (cont.)

Five Stages of the Writing Process - *details*

1. Brainstorm

As you Brainstorm and complete your Topic Wheels, use the opportunity to plan how you will engage your readers. Think about the famous person you are writing about and imagine them as a real person. What was their day-to-day life like? What brought him or her joy? What did he or she look forward to? What things made life difficult? What made life fun? Write down as many ideas related to the topic as you can think of, then choose your five best ideas to complete your Topic Wheel.

2. First Draft

Use your completed topic wheels as a scaffolding to develop a first draft of each Topic Paragraph. Be sure to open each of the expanded paragraphs with an interesting topic sentence that introduces the reader to the paragraph's topic. Present your ideas in a sequence that is logical. Finally, at the end of your paragraph, craft a single closing sentence that will leave your reader with an idea to continue thinking about.

When you have completed the first draft of your Topic Paragraphs, develop the first draft of your opening and closing paragraphs in a similar way.

Remember, the best way to get your First Draft started is to JUST START WRITING! Even if it's not exactly what you want to say, words on paper are much easier to edit than words that are stuck in your head.

3. Conference

Now that you have the First Draft of your complete essay, an Opening Paragraph, three Topic Paragraphs, and a Closing Paragraph, make a careful check of spelling and grammar, and then get a second opinion. Having someone else read your essay before it is done is an excellent way to find out how well you are communicating your ideas and if you are capturing the reader's interest.

4. Edit/Polish

After conferencing, be open to input and decide how you want to incorporate any comments from your reader. Make your changes and read your essay again, out loud if possible. While reading, check your spelling and grammar one more time and make any needed changes.

5. Final Draft

So far, you have Brainstormed, Drafted, Conferenced, and Polished. The hard work is done! Now re-write your essay using your best penmanship and make it beautiful for others to see. Even if you don't think your writing is great, this will be great practice, and others will appreciate the effort and care that you put into your work.

Grading Guidelines

Full points are awarded for complete and creative work that goes beyond the basic requirements. No points are awarded when the work has not been done. Know your student and individualize the following grading guidelines by awarding points accordingly.

Reading .... **5 Points**

Character Lexicon...... **5 Points**

Comprehension .... **5 Points**

Writing .... **10 Points** (See below)

Total................................. **25 Points**

Grading Your Student's Writing
When evaluating your student's writing, use the following guidelines:

Accomplished ....(10 points)
> Creatively focuses on the topic
> Uses logical progression of ideas to develop and supports topic with details
> Varies sentence structure
> Uses interesting transitions and strong word choice
> Mature understanding of writing conventions

Proficient ....(8 points)
> Focuses on topic and includes adequate support
> Uses logical progression of ideas to develop and loosely supports topic
> Some varied sentence structure
> Transitions and word choice are adequate but not creative
> General understanding of writing conventions

Basic ....(6 points)
> Topic is addressed, but unclear
> Lacks logical progression of ideas and support is weak
> Sentences are stagnant and uninteresting
> Lack of transitions and average word choice
> Partial understanding of writing conventions

Limited ....(4 points)
> Topic may be mentioned, but not clearly addressed and supported loosely
> Organization pattern is weak
> Writing contains sentence fragments and run-on's
> Poor transitions and word choice
> Definite misunderstanding of writing conventions

Poor ....(2 points)
> Topic is not addressed or clearly supported
> Organizational pattern is lacking
> Sentence structure is insufficient
> Non-existent transitions and inappropriate word choice
> Frequent errors in basic writing conventions

Let's Get Started

Assignment Checklist

Reading assignments: ***Who Was Jacques Cousteau?***

Supplemental Reading: ***Manfish: A Story of Jacques Cousteau*** — by Jennifer Berne

ASSIGNMENT	POINTS	TEACHER COMMENTS	GRADE

Section 1: *Who Was Jacques Cousteau? — Chapter 4: Underwater Breathing*

○ Reading .... /5
○ Character Lexicon .... /5
○ Comprehension .... /5
○ Writing (10 possible)
  ○ Brainstorm .... /3
  ○ Topic Wheel .... /3
  ○ First Draft .... /4

/ 25

Section 2: *Chapters 5: France at War — Chapter 8: A Life at Sea*

○ Reading .... /5
○ Character Lexicon .... /5
○ Comprehension .... /5
○ Writing (10 possible)
  ○ Brainstorm .... /3
  ○ Topic Wheel .... /3
  ○ First Draft .... /4

/ 25

Section 3: *Chapters 9: A Life Under the Sea — Chapter 11: Future Generations*

○ Reading .... /5
○ Character Lexicon .... /5
○ Comprehension .... /5
○ Writing (10 possible)
  ○ Brainstorm .... /3
  ○ Topic Wheel .... /3
  ○ First Draft .... /4

/ 25

Section 4: *Opening — Closing — Final Draft*

○ Opening First Draft .... /5
○ Closing First Draft .... /5
○ Final Draft .... /15

/ 25

Final Score / 100

Essay Diagram

Use this diagram to help you pace your essay.

Section 1–3: Write the first drafts of your 3 Topic Paragraphs.

Section 4: Write the first drafts of your opening and closing paragraphs.
Compile your 5 paragraphs into your final essay.

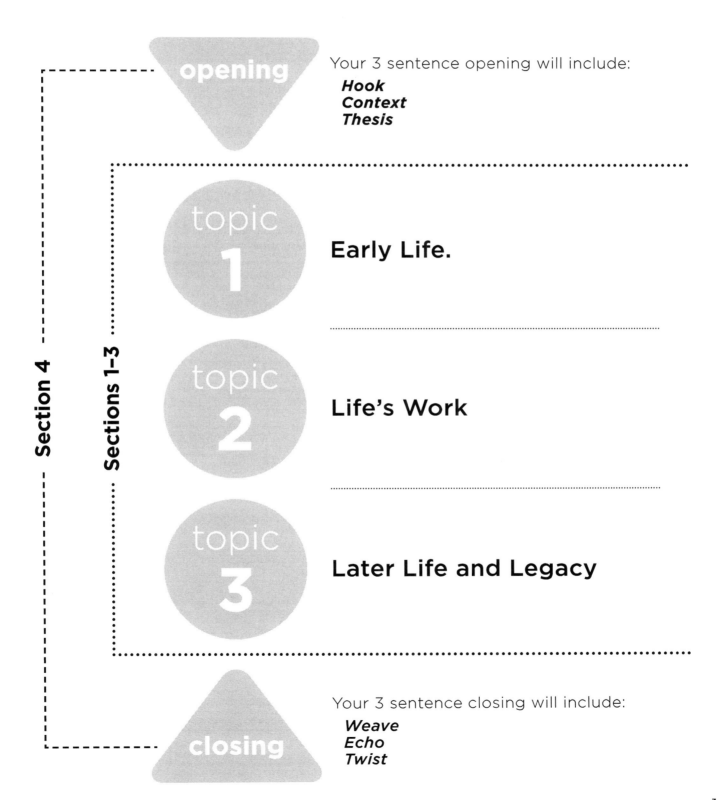

opening

Your 3 sentence opening will include:
Hook
Context
Thesis

topic 1

Early Life.

topic 2

Life's Work

topic 3

Later Life and Legacy

closing

Your 3 sentence closing will include:
Weave
Echo
Twist

Section 4

Sections 1–3

Section 1 » **Early Life**

Read » Who Was Jacques Coustea? — Chapter 4

**Character Lexicon > ** Definitions

Use a dictionary to define the following character traits:

sickly	linger	pioneer	innovative	inventor

1. _____
_____
_____

2. _____
_____
_____

3. _____
_____
_____

4. _____
_____
_____

5. _____
_____
_____

Character Lexicon > Sentences

Use each character trait in a complete and original sentence about the person you are studying. Use your definitions and be sure to incorporate specific details from the reading.

1.

2.

3.

4.

5.

Comprehension Questions

Answer the following questions using complete sentences.

1. How was Jacques Cousteau punished when he refused to ride horses at summer camp?

2. How did Cousteau spend the time sailing across the Atlantic Ocean when his family moved to New York City?

3. What item helped Cousteau to become less shy?

4. What happened when Cousteau borrowed his father's car to attend a wedding?

5. What did Cousteau's friend, Tailliez, use for swimming equipment?

6. What did Cousteau, Tailliez, and Frédéric Dumas call themselves?

7. How did Cousteau make his camera waterproof?

begin topic paragraph 1 »

Writing > Brainstorm

Use this page to write down words or phrases
that support **Topic 1** on the next page.

How many ideas can you think of?

Topic 1:

1. _____

2. _____

3. _____

4. _____

5. _____

6. _____

7. _____

8. _____

9. _____

10. _____

_____

_____

_____

_____

_____

_____

Writing > Topic Wheel 1

Use this topic wheel to help you plan **Topic Paragraph 1**.

Choose the five best ideas from your brainstorm on the previous page and write each into one of the spokes below.

Each spoke will be made into one complete sentence of **Topic Paragraph 1**.

topic
1

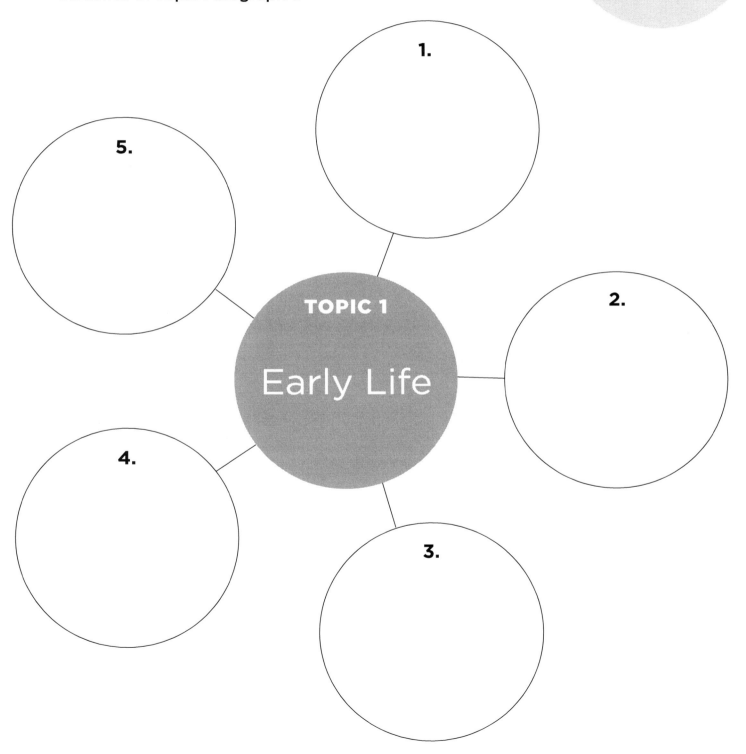

1.

5.

TOPIC 1

Early Life

2.

4.

3.

Writing > Topic Paragraph 1: First Draft

1. Begin your paragraph with an opening sentence that introduces your subject.

2. Use the five ideas from **Topic Wheel 1** to create the five main sentences of your paragraph.

3. Close your paragraph with a strong clincher.

> *Conference, edit,* and *polish* your First Draft in this section.
>
> **Complete the Final Draft in Section 4.**

1. Opening sentence

2. Body sentences

Writing > Topic Paragraph 1: First Draft (cont.)

_____

_____

_____

_____

_____

_____

_____

_____

_____

_____

_____

_____

3. Closing sentence

_____

_____

_____

_____

Section 2 » Life's Work

Read » Chapters 5 — 8

Character Lexicon > Definitions

Use a dictionary to define the following character traits:

patriotic	resistant	Imaginative	celebrity	devoted

1.

2.

3.

4.

5.

Character Lexicon > Sentences

Use each character trait in a complete and original sentence about the person you are studying. Use your definitions and be sure to incorporate specific details from the reading.

1.

2.

3.

4.

5.

Comprehension Questions

Answer the following questions using complete sentences.

1. How did Cousteau use his skill of underwater breathing to help his ship in the war?

2. How did Cousteau put his photography hobby to good use as part of the French Resistance?

3. What did Cousteau help to create along with Émile Gagnan?

4. What group did the Sea Musketeers found in the French Navy?

5. How deep did Cousteau make it when he was testing the limits of his Aqua-Lung?

6. What did Cousteau find off the coast of Marseille?

7. What awards did Cousteau's film, The Silent World, win?

begin topic paragraph 2 »

Writing > Brainstorm

Use this page to write down words or phrases
that support **Topic 2** on the next page.

How many ideas can you think of?

Topic 2: _____

1. _____

2. _____

3. _____

4. _____

5. _____

6. _____

7. _____

8. _____

9. _____

10. _____

_____

_____

_____

_____

_____

_____

Writing > Topic Wheel 2

Use this topic wheel to help you plan **Topic Paragraph 2**.

Choose the five best ideas from your brainstorm on the previous page and write each into one of the spokes below.

Each spoke will be made into one complete sentence of **Topic Paragraph 2**.

topic
2

Writing > Topic Paragraph 1: First Draft

1. Begin your paragraph with an opening sentence that introduces your subject.

2. Use the five ideas from **Topic Wheel 2** to create the five main sentences of your paragraph.

3. Close your paragraph with a strong clincher.

Conference, edit, and *polish* your First Draft in this section.

Complete the Final Draft in Section 4.

1. Opening sentence

2. Body sentences

Writing > Topic Paragraph 2: First Draft (cont.)

3. Closing sentence

Section 3 » **Later Life and Legacy**

Read » Chapters 9 — 11

Character Lexicon > Definitions

Use a dictionary to define the following character traits:

advocate	vocal	adventurous	resilient	affectionate

1. _____

_____

_____

2. _____

_____

_____

3. _____

_____

_____

4. _____

_____

_____

5. _____

_____

_____

Character Lexicon > Sentences

Use each character trait in a complete and original sentence about the person you are studying. Use your definitions and be sure to incorporate specific details from the reading.

1. _____

2. _____

3. _____

4. _____

5. _____

Comprehension Questions

Answer the following questions using complete sentences.

1. What job did Cousteau take after leaving the French Navy?

2. Where did Cousteau live during his experiments in 1962?

3. What were the problems with Deep Cabin, the deepest habitat Cousteau built underwater?

4. What were the side effects of the men who were breathing 98% helium aboard the Conshelf III?

5. What was Cousteau's first television special and who was it narrated by?

6. How did the Calypso escape the fighting armies during the Six Day-War?

7. Why did Cousteau establish the Cousteau Society?

begin topic paragraph 3 »

Writing > Brainstorm

Use this page to write down words or phrases that support **Topic 3** on the next page.

How many ideas can you think of?

Topic 3:

1.

2.

3.

4.

5.

6.

7.

8.

9.

10.

Writing > Topic Wheel 3

Use this topic wheel to help you plan **Topic Paragraph 3**.

Choose the five best ideas from your brainstorm on the previous page and write each into one of the spokes below.

Each spoke will be made into one complete sentence of **Topic Paragraph 3**.

topic 3

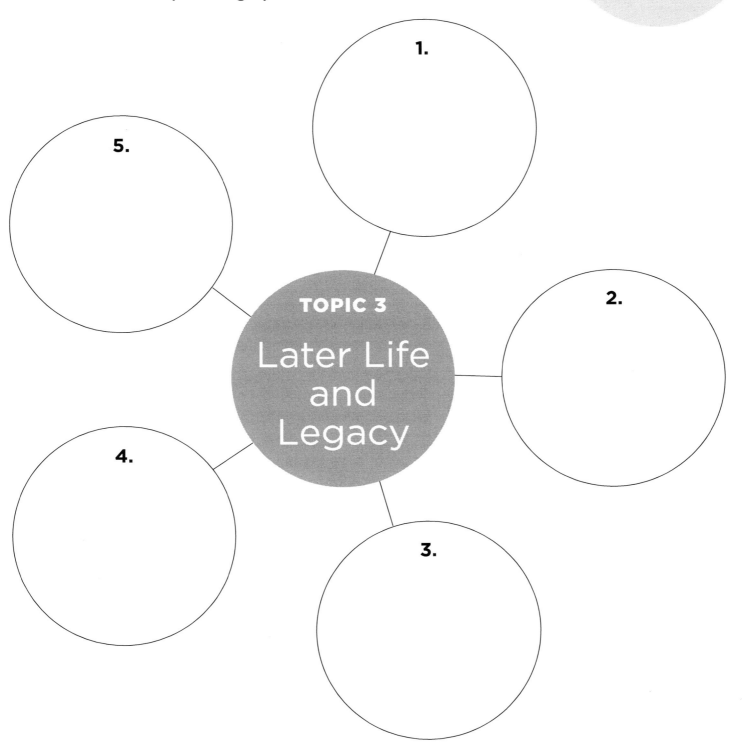

1.

2.

3.

4.

5.

TOPIC 3
Later Life and Legacy

Writing > Topic Paragraph 3: First Draft

1. Begin your paragraph with an opening sentence that introduces your subject.
2. Use the five ideas from **Topic Wheel 3** to create the five main sentences of your paragraph.
3. Close your paragraph with a strong clincher.

Conference, edit, and *polish* your First Draft in this section.

Complete the Final Draft in Section 4.

1. Opening sentence

2. Body sentences

Writing > Topic Paragraph 3: First Draft (cont.)

topic
3

3. Closing sentence

Section 4 » **Final Essay**

Writing > Final Essay

Congratulations!

You've done the hard work of writing the core content of your essay.

On the following pages:

1   **» Write your 3 sentence opening paragraph**

After writing the first draft of your opening paragraph begin the first draft of your closing paragraph.

2   **» Write your 3 sentence closing paragraph**

After writing the first draft of your closing paragraph conference, edit, and polish both your opening and closing paragraphs, then move on to the final step.

3   **» Bring all the pieces together**

Combine your opening paragraph, your 3 topic paragraphs, and your closing paragraph into one final essay.

Writing > Opening Paragraph: First Draft

1. Begin your Opening Paragraph with a **Hook** that grabs the reader's attention.

2. Use a **Context Sentence** to move to the **Thesis**.

3. Close your paragraph with a **Thesis** that introduces your main idea .

Writing > Closing Paragraph: First Draft

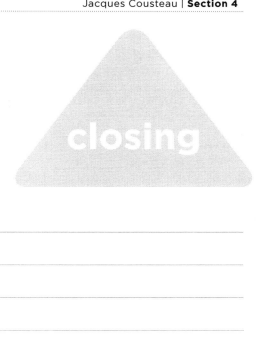

closing

1. Begin your Closing Paragraph with a **Weave** that begins to close your essay.

2. Use an **Echo** to move your reader to the **Twist**.

3. Close your paragraph with a **Twist** that will keep your readers thinking.

Writing > Final Draft

Once you have **conferenced**, **edited**, and **polished** your 5 paragraphs, *opening – topic 1 – topic 2 – topic 3 – closing,* complete your final draft by combining them here, in the correct order, using your best penmanship.

Writing > Final Draft (cont.)

FINAL
DRAFT

Writing > Final Draft (cont.)

Writing > Final Draft (cont.)

Section 5 » **Final Project**

Assignment Options

Following are suggestions for creative projects and further research:

1. Ask a parent to help you research Cousteau's ship *Calypso*. Build a model or create a picture of the ship using collage, watercolor, colored pencils, or another method of your choosing.

2. Take a trip to a local beach, lake, or other body of water. Find interesting stones, sticks, shells, or other items, and research the species that live in the area.

3. Use the timeline in the back of *Who Was Jacques Cousteau?* and select what you believe are the most important events in his life. Draw a picture for each event and present them to family or friends.

4. Research the ship *Calypso* and make a map of the rooms on board, writing details of what each room was used for.

5. Choose another great explorer of the world's oceans and write a short, one-page paper on them, then, present what you find to friends and family. Some examples are: Marco Polo, Francis Drake, Ferdinand Magellan, and Amerigo Vespucci.

Need a little inspiration?

Scan here to view our student project gallery!